Broken Voi(

by

Alan Peters

Table of Contents

Performing Broken Voices

All performance rights are held by Alan Peters Freelancer.

In order to perform this play applications must be made by email to

abpeters@abpetersfreelancer.co.uk

Conditions are purchase of a minimum of ten copies of the script – one for each cast member, one for the director and one for the tech team.

At the time of writing, the cost per performance is £30, or £100 for four performances. No part of the script may be cut or changed without prior permission of the author (contactable on the above email address). The exception to this are the songs, which can be changed subject to the Director's discretion.

Cast (in order of speaking)

Seb

Will

Ben

Ed

Alex

Jasmin

Georgia

Cam

The cast are aged somewhere between 11 and 16.

Synopsis

Broken Voices was first performed at St Augustine's Vault at the 2010 Edinburgh Fringe. It earned numerous five star reviews and its short run almost sold out.

The story revolves around a group of children or young people put into detention on some kind of school trip. We never really know what they have done.

Each character's story is told, interwoven with dialogue between the group. When Cam, a Mephistophelean figure, arrives discontent turns to violence.

The play seeks to explore themes of bullying by teachers towards their pupils, and how other adults can have a negative influence on young people's lives. A surreal quality is sought in the production, and neither dialogue not events are meant to reflect the real way young people speak.

Their world is captured in the language of Enid Blyton and Boy Scouts. Only occasionally does it come close to being real to life.

The play lends itself ideally to small school or youth productions. It fits ideally with GCSE drama work, drama club productions and serious plays that schools might look to do with their most able and keen actors, rather than a large-scale production.

It lends itself to performances in small spaces such as a studio or classroom. Tech is straightforward and can be developed by students or adult directors.

Although serious themes of bullying and violence are tackled, the surreal quality of the writing and the lack of any sexual references or strong language make it ideal for use in schools.

Act One

SETTING: A largish room; uncomfortable chairs are scattered around – there could be bunk beds in corners. A table is on one side, which is often used for sitting on. There is rubbish everywhere – sweet papers especially, and clothes scattered untidily

Seb sings a version of 'Where is love?' It breaks down towards the end.

Seb: I want another go. I want another go. Mum. Tell them.

He sits. The others look. There is silence.

Will: I want another go...mum.

Ben: Please mum, make them let me have another go.

Ed: Please mum...

Alex: Yes mum, you can make them do anything.

Ed: Go on mum...

Pause. For all pauses, form a tableau

Ben: I'm bored.

Will: You're always bored.

Ed: Mum, stop me being bored.

Seb: Leave me

Ed: Piss off.

Ben: It's the thing, being bored. 'You're always bored' they say. Well, so what. You'd be bored. It's the same every day. Get up, go to school. Sit there, listening. English, Maths, Science, History, Rugby with Piggins. 'Get changed you lot, get out on that pitch' It's freezing half the time. 'Pass the ball, pass the ball – you dropped it Cooper. Why did you drop it

Cooper?' And you want to tell him that it's freezing and your fingers are falling off and actually you'd rather be anywhere doing anything else but you just say, 'Sorry Sir'. 'Sorry Sir – we're all sorry. Sorry you're out here, spoiling this practice boy. ' Every week. 'Right boys, time for a match' he says, grinning, like it's Christmas or something. Look at me. I'm expected to tackle him (points at Will). Yeh. 'You missed the tackle boy, you can't tackle with one hand'. 'Think I'm stupid' I want to say, 'Think I want that landing on top of me?' Jesus. But you don't say anything, apart from 'Sorry sir.' Then you go home, and do your homework, and go to scouts or whatever it is that night. You get back, and go to bed. 'I'm bored' 'You can't be bored' they say 'you go to the best school (and don't forget the sacrifice we're making, your sister didn't get this), you go to football and scouts and swimming. 'But I'm shit at swimming'

I want to say. I don't. 'You're going on this trip or that trip – how can you be bored?' they say. 'You get too much, that's your trouble...' Yeah. Here I am.

Will: Isn't it time you phoned mummy? Might you want her to come and clean your teeth?

Alex: Heat your hot water bottle?

Ed: Wipe your bottom?

Will: Perhaps you'd like to sing to her?

Alex: A lullaby. (*Sings*) Hush little baby, don't say a word

Mama's going to buy you a mocking bird

(*they all join in, except Seb*)
And if that mocking bird don't sing

Mummy's going to buy you everything

Seb (*Obviously heard this before*) Get lost...

Ben: He can't help it. 'Ask your mummy...what will mummy say?' 'Voice of an angel' Mr Hardcastle said in assembly. That went down well. In the early rounds, the teachers made such a thing of it. 'Our own star' they said in assembly. And he had to go on the stage and perform in front of everybody. This lot were bad enough, but the Removes murdered him. He couldn't understand why. I went to his house once. It's not that we're mates or anything – no way. But I went around and he has absolutely everything. The latest. And his mum... We got in from school, right – she carried his bags from the car. Made him a sandwich – and me, stood over him while he ate it. Brought us drinks – 'What do you want darling? Good job I'm not diabetic, and he just sort of sat there, eating and drinking and ignoring me. We went to his room... I watched him play Premiership Manager for two hours. *(mimes taking the PlayStation, having a go, having it taken away again)* 'You'll spoil my record'. Clothes – folded *(smiles)* immaculate, but weird. He'd got all the right posters, but it was too neat. And when my dad collected me, his mum didn't even know my name.

Seb: I couldn't help it that I was good. Did they want me to be rubbish?

Ed: *Walks across to Seb, pings his ear.*

Will: It's your fault we're here.

Alex: We could have been singing around the camp fire.

(They look at each other, and grin)

Ben: I didn't even want to be in this group.

Seb: Nor did I.

Will: They don't do one with mummies.

Alex: Mums and toddlers.

Pause

Seb: Later, when they're not expecting it, I'll come to their beds and cut their heads open. I can, if I want to. I'll shove their pillows over their faces, push their blankets into their mouths. They can't imagine – they're so small and insignificant –Just because I'm good at something; just because my parents actually support me – they envy what I can do; but they don't know half of it; if they could see what I can think, imagine what I can achieve...Lights half blind me, and the noise of the audience as they whip them up – 'Seb-by, Seb-by'; the orchestra plays and I start. Mess it up, I was told, that'll get them on your side, make a big story of it...use your acting skills they told me...do they think I can't sing a song? Do they really think I would cry like that if it wasn't an act?

Pause

Ed: Miss Winstone – can you do my life jacket up.

Alex: Thank you Miss Winstone I feel very secure now.

Ed: Would you like some help with yours Miss Winstone? I'm sure Alex would assist you.

Alex: Yes Miss, would you like me to?

Ben: Be quiet you cheeky boys.

Ed: Cheeky Miss, that's us.

Alex: But we thought you liked a bit of cheek Miss.

Ben: And just what are you insinuating?

Alex: That's a long word Miss, don't think I completely understand what that means Miss.

Ed: Could you explain it to us Miss? We're all ears.

Ben: I'm warning you boys.

Alex: Is that a final warning Miss Winstone?

Ed: Or a first warning? Because it's important to understand the difference.

Ben: A FINAL warning.

Alex: It's final Ed. That could mean trouble.

Ed: BIG trouble.

Ben: I'm warning you boys...

Ed: Another warning Miss?

Alex: A final final warning...

Ben: That I shall report your behaviour to Mr Sharp.

Alex: Oh no!

Ed: I bet you will, miss.

Alex: And he'd listen to you...

Ed: In a 'flash' Miss...

Alex: Straight away or later tonight...are you his kind, Miss?

Ed: I think you'd like to be...but not much hope there...

(They erupt into giggles)

Will: And we've all been here since dinner.

Ben: Missing the camp fire.

Will: Yeah. Still, *(silly baby voice)* the smoke would hurt your voice and what would mummy say then?

Ben: *(Sings and coughs through a song)*

On Ilkley Moor bar t'at *(where's that?)*

On Ilkley Moor bar t'at *(where's that?)*

On Ilkley Moor bar t'at

Pause. There is a banging at the window.

Jasmin: Let us in.

Will: What do you want?

Jasmin: Just open the door.

She sneaks in with Georgia.

Will: What have brought her for?

Jasmin: *Shrugs* It stinks in here.

Ed: *pointing* him.

Jasmin: It's all of you.

Will: Go then.

Jasmin: Yeah, yeah. You'd be disappointed.

Georgia: We should be at the fire.

Jasmin: You get back if you like. Little puppy dog.

Alex: Woof Woof.

Georgia: You want to be with her and not against her, to begin with. I was waiting for the teacher and she sat next to me. I didn't know what to think, because usually she hates me. 'Georgia' she said, all friendly like, 'can I sit here today?' I just nodded? 'Won't Melanie mind, you always sit together.' We'd been together since Infants. 'It's up to you.' So, she says to me, 'The thing is, Georgia, I'm really on a final warning. If I get suspended again, they'll kick me out, after last time. If I can sit next to you, I can do my work, and I won't get so distracted.' So, every English lesson...then she asks, really carefully like, whether we can work together in Science. She says she's rubbish at it, and perhaps I can help her. The thing is, she's fun to be with. She's always cracking jokes, Then Melanie and me had this huge row– a pencil crayon she leant me, Jasmin borrowed it, and dropped it and cracked the lead. Melanie said it was ruined and it wasn't mine to give out to others, especially Jasmin Lewis, and I told her to grow up and it was only a stupid pencil. Next thing, Jasmin gets me at break, and she's with all her gang and they say I can join it if I want to. But I have to pass an initiation. She's written a letter, made out it's to Melanie and signed it from a boy. It was outrageous, I tell you. But I have to make up with Melanie, and get invited back to hers, then leave the letter where her mum will find it. Melanie's mum's one of these religious kinds, and I know she'll go mad if she finds it. But I do it anyway, and here's the final bit, I have to tell Melanie what I've done – then I've passed the initiation. Now, I sit by myself in English, and Science and everything, because Melanie won't talk to me, nor will my old mates, and my new sisters *–shakes her head.* But here's the trick, see. *(Sarcastic)* Jasmin, you see, clearly, deep down, wants to be my friend –

so if I stick with her everywhere, sometime, eventually, she'll see the light.

Jasmin: She's a cow. You should meet my mum if you want an experience. ... but I can't get it from her, because she's just a stick. I've got a sister who's 17 and she's like a twin with my mum. They even dress the same. Dad calls me Podge – from when I was a baby –Look at me. Emma is so good at everything. 'Why can't you be like your sister' mum says. Because I'm not my sister.

I'm on a diet. It's not working. Look at them, they think I'm so gross.

Hello Sebastian, how are you tonight?

Seb: OK

Jasmin: Hey, Georgia?

Georgia: Get real.

Will: It's not you he needs.

Ed and Alex: *Gin Gan Gooly etc*

Ging gan goolie-goolie-goolie-goolie wotcha

Ging gan goo, ging gang goo.

Ging gan goolie-goolie-goolie-goolie wotcha

Ging gan goo, ging gang goo

Seb: You shouldn't be in our dorm.

Will: What's it to you?

Seb: I don't mind – I'm just saying...

Will: Well don't.

Pause

Jasmin: This is good.

Georgia: Yeah.

Ed: Let's party...

Ben: Music, dance.

Will: We haven't got any music.

Pause

Look at them. What a pair, whatever you want to call them. At my dad's...Can't you clear off? OK then. Hey Sebastian...like your mum? Is she Sebastian? Is that why you always need her? Eh, Sebastian – eh? Come on then, come on then...Yeah. What are you looking at? It was his weekend...the first time I saw it. What are you looking at? Do you want some? Get off – you're just fat tarts – that's all. They're so immature. Fancy yourselves girls don't you – but you're just little kids. You think that you know so much, but you don't. *(Pause - antagonism towards Ed, who just holds up his hand)*

I was nine, Sara was seven. dad's weekend. Saturday afternoon. supposed to be going out somewhere – the zoo probably – how many times can you see a cage full of monkeys, even when you're nine. *(He goes to the window)*

Listen to them. Out there, singing round a camp fire. I don't care that we're here, if I'm honest. Listen to them singing – little kids who know nothing. CAN'T YOU DO SOMETHING? *(His scream is met by no movement)* We couldn't go. Dad couldn't drive. He couldn't walk or stand either. Is there a problem Sebastian? Is that why you're staring at me? *(He threatens)*

Horse racing on Sky. Sarah was too young for the games he got for us.

If we don't have any music then Sebastian can sing. That's what you do, Sebby boy, sing. Voice of an angel, so I've heard. So, sing. Come on, I want to dance. We can have our own disco – you sing and dance with them. Eh? Sing boy. Sing, Sing, Sing. Dance – *He grabs Jasmin*!

She just said she had nothing to do – *(he throws Jasmin across the room, walks across to her and raises his hand very high and threateningly)*

Jasmin: Emma can dance – she does tap and modern and folk and ballet. Emma goes out. She's alright. And my mum goes with her –acting like she's still a kid.

Seb: It's in my head *(Sings)* All in the merry month of May, when the green buds they were swellin; Young William Green on his death bed lay, for love of Barbry Allen.

Georgia: Are you alright?

Jasmin: Course I'm alright. Can't you see I'm alright? Anyway, why don't you just clear off outside. I don't want you following me everywhere

Pause.

Ben: What time's lights out?

Seb: I want to go home.

Jasmin: To mummy.

Ben: Mummy will look after you Sebby.

Jasmin: Put you to bed.

Seb: I just want to go home.

Will: Shut up.

Seb: Please.

Georgia: Shall I get the teacher?

Jasmin: Yeah, go and get him, and we can lock the door when you leave.

Pause. Alex begins to hum or whistle 'Gin Gan Goolie', they ignore him.

ED AS TEACHER: What are you girls doing in here?

Will: Not what you think.

Ed: We didn't do anything. Sir.

Ben: Come on sir, *(He stops, as if he has gone too far)*

Will: Yeah let us out to the campfire. It sounds such fun.

Alex: It wasn't them, though, it was me and Ed...

Ed: That's right sir...

Alex: It's not fair...

Ed: How's Miss Winstone?

Jasmin: Come on sir, how is she?

Ed: I'm sure she'll tell you...if you ask nicely...

Ben: Sir, your shoe laces are undone. You might fall over. Do them up then. No sir, your laces. Do them up. Now. Sir? Get down and do them up. Now. Get down and do them up. How dare you be so damned impudent. When I want your advice on my appearance, you rude little child, I'll ask. But until then, you just do as you are told. Sir, I'm not doing up your shoe laces. Oh yes you are. Sir *(shakes head)*. Are you disobeying a clear instruction? No sir. Then do them up. I can't sir. Why not? Not allowed to. Get to my office. Now. Cooper. You really are the most disagreeable child in this school. I'm tempted to haul you in front of the headmaster – let him deal with you. OK Sir. What did you say? *(Stronger)* OK Sir. After school, back here, straight away. I don't care if your parents have to wait until tomorrow to collect you. You will come here, and by god you'll learn to do as you are told.

Ed: I'm sure that Benjamin is exaggerating...

Georgia: Thirty minutes I waited, and he was too terrified to come to school today...

Ed: Mr Sharp is certainly strict, we often say Sharp by name and sharp by tongue

(ALL – HA HA HA)

But he always puts the interests of the children first...

Mr Sharp, a word...

Will: Absolutely not Headmaster, I don't know what the child is talking about...

Ben: Cooper – here...now. You little liar, Cooper, are you listening to me, Cooper – COME HERE – let me look at you. Why are you wearing that badge

Cooper? It's for charity Sir. Is it school uniform,

Cooper? No, sir, but I thought... *(He mimes tearing*

his tie) What are you doing? Going to tell that to your

parents Cooper?

Alex: You've got your elbows on the table, Cooper.

(As they speak they encircle him)

Georgia: Don't hold your knife and fork like that,

Cooper. What do you think you are?

Jasmin: How were you brought up, Cooper

Will: Talking in Assembly, Cooper...

Ed: I've had a complaint about you from the Games

teachers Cooper – skiving showers...why's that,

Cooper?

Jasmin: Call this Homework Cooper?

Alex: You've got your mates into trouble this time

Cooper.

Seb: What are you talking about Cooper.

ALL: Shut Up.

Will: If you can imagine what it's like seeing your little sister wet herself with fear, and still you want to see your dad, because he's your dad.

He sings. She'll be coming 'round the mountain when she comes. (Yee Hah!)

She'll be coming 'round the mountain when she comes. (Yee Hah!)

She'll be coming 'round the mountain,

She'll be coming 'round the mountain,

She'll be coming 'round the mountain when she comes. (Yee Hah!)

(The girls join in)

She'll be riding six white horses when she comes. (Whoa back!)

(The remainder join in)

Oh, we'll kill the old red rooster when she comes.

(hack hack!)

Cameron Enters.

Cameron: Well sir, is this where all the naughty boys and girls get sent? Sounds more like fun than a punishment. I've got my bag sir, and I can guarantee to take on board what you've said. Absolutely. 100 per cent. Good evening everyone, Cameron is my name, but most people call me Cam. Only arrived today, and in trouble already. What a little rascal I am. Do you know, Sir, I sense a bit of an atmosphere in here.

END OF ACT ONE

Act Two

The Same Place

Cam: I've got my bag sir, and I can guarantee to take on board what you've said. Absolutely. 100 per cent. Good evening everyone, Cameron is my name, but most people call me Cam. Only arrived today, and in trouble already. What a little rascal I am. Do you know, Sir, I sense a bit of an atmosphere in here.

Pause

Will: It was always my sister most, but sometimes me as well. He doesn't hit me now.

Cam: Hey, you're not, you can't be can you? Yes, Yes, you are. My god, Jesus, wow that is amazing. It is you isn't it. From TV? Guys, please, tell me, is that the boy, you know, from the Talent Show – what's it called. Can't remember, never mind. It is –

Sebastian – 'Seb-by, Seb-by'. And Sebastian goes to

our school? To my new school? Is it, is it a school for

superstars – gosh I bet you're all superstars in your

little ways. My word. I'm just so impressed. Hey,

Sebastian – Seb, *(aside)* do you mind - is that OK? -

can I, please – can I have your autograph? Just wait

till I tell my mother about this. Jesus Christ Almighty.

Wow. Just. I mean I know you messed up in the final

– hey guys did you see that – I bet you were glued to

your screens – but even so. A star – here. In my

dorm.

Will: What are you saying?

Cam: Did I say something wrong? Did I?

Georgia: We've got to go.

Cam: No don't – how can we party without girls?

(to Georgia) How did she draw you in, eh? Be my friend, forget the others? But I think, Georgia, that you're stronger than that.

Georgia: I am.

Cam: Well, well, Jasmin, my old chucker. That wasn't the plan.

Jasmin: How do you know my name?

Pause

Cam: Friendly lot, aren't you?

Will: Shut up, before I smack you.

Cam: Yes, you'd do that, I think.

Will: I would, you're right.

Cam: No, wait. It's interesting I think. You see, you'd hit him *(points at Seb)* just like that – I can see it in your eyes – and the girls, yeah, no respect there...

Will: Watch it...

Cam: But not the others – I wonder why – you're nearly the biggest...is he bigger than you, Ed? And, I think, me...I've nothing to worry about. No.

Jasmin: You're really weird.

Georgia: He's not...

Jasmin: He is...

Ed: What about this party. *(Nothing happens)*

Cam: That's right boys, you do what is right for you, there's no need to rush. You were rushed, weren't you Ben? And now it's just not right, I think, that you don't really want to be here, at this school. So why did you come – Ben?

Will: Yeah, Ben.

Ben: I don't know what you're talking about. I don't know even who you are.

Cam: Are you in detention again Cooper? That's the third time this term. What is it this time Cooper? Late for lessons. Punctuality. It isn't much to ask.

Ben: I was talking to Mrs Laidlaw Sir.

Cam: There's always an *excuse isn't there Cooper. You are such a disgusting, snivelling little wretch. You are pathetic. Do you know that?

Ben: *(joining in)* *excuse isn't there Cooper. You are such a disgusting, snivelling little wretch. You are pathetic. Do you know that? You can't speak to me like that. Yes, I can, I can speak to you exactly as I wish. I can do to you exactly what I want. When I want, and how I want. I'll tell my parents. I bet you will. You little sneak, Cooper. Do you know what, eh? You're not the sort of boy we want at this school.

You haven't got the class. You'll never fit in here. I will, Sir, and I do...

(Ben mimes being poked backwards, arms out)

Ed: Listen to me, you foul child...

Cam: The smell of fish for lunch, stale coffee and sweat mingled with after shave, expensive but sweet and cloying...

Seb: Sebastian – you sang so beautifully this morning...

Georgia: He sneaks up to the huts so we can't see him, but the boys have look outs, and when they see him coming they stop what they are doing and pretend to talk...

Jasmin: He hides beneath the window thinking we don't know he's there...waiting to catch us doing something wrong...

Will: There was this boy in the class, and his dad died suddenly

Alex: He's been gone for three months, you have to move on...

Ben: And he stood there over me, breathing hard, and I knew that there was nothing he could do. He could say what he liked...but nothing he could do...

Ed: Oh yes there is, Cooper...

Ben: No sir, there's not.

Cam: So There we are. We'll see. *(Pause)* Who's it going to be, eh, Seb? Too soon. So, girls – how's it going. You're looking good. Yeah, nice.

Jasmin: You're weird.

Cam: I am.

Will: Raises his hand, just like that. She looked so scared. He doesn't do it to me, not any more.

Seb: I told her that I didn't want to come here. Do the test, Seb, she said, and we'll see. I've got you a tutor. Just for maths Seb. YOU ARE TRYING SAYING NO TO HER. And the singing - might get you a scholarship; we'll be making a big sacrifice...but I don't want to go mum.

Ben: Cooper! Do you call this homework, Cooper? Look at it. I'm going to tear it up in front of your eyes. Rubbish. That's what that is. Absolute rubbish. In the bin, where it belongs. Tell your parents about that, eh Cooper? Oh, they'll be glad enough to hear the truth about your excuse for work. Every maths lesson the same. Set it out properly, Cooper.

Cam: Must be tough, eh, Ben. Shame. Want some chocolate? I've got some here somewhere. Loads actually. Midnight feasts eh chaps? Iced buns and

ginger beer and lashings of cream soda...

Will: What the...

Cam: Rather an adventure this, isn't it? Here it is.

Yes, a bar for each of you...oh dash, one short.

Jasmin, can I ask...would you mind...I can see that

you would probably prefer...but to me, pretty as a

picture. Don't you agree boys, pretty as can be.

Jasmin: I look in the mirror sometimes, and I see my

mum and sister.

Cam: Have a bar – cheer yourself up. Have mine.

They eat, each in their own thoughts.

Jasmin: She follows me everywhere now. If I go, she

goes. I get to school and she's waiting. Miss Georgia

Porgia – Miss Podge...He doesn't mean any harm.

And Mum, and Emma, maybe I can go to when I'm

older. a three...'The Podge Sisters' and dad can collect us after the party and we'll sing all the way home. The three of us, in the back of the car.

Cam: Who's up for a jolly good party game – that will cheer us up. Charades. That's a good one. Ben – fancy a go? Will...no. Girls? Boys, yes...but can you keep it clean? No, Seb. Go on Seb...

Ben: Yeah go on Seb...

Will: Your turn...

Ben: Come on Seb...give mummy a call if you like...

Seb: I don't want to do the test and I don't want a tutor and I don't want to be Oliver and I don't want to go to that stupid show.

Will: Do it!

Cam: Me first. Now, let's think... *(He mimes 'Britain's got talent' and the others join in and guess. They stop, as if the teacher is about to enter)*

Georgia: We better go...

Jasmin: Yeah...

Alex: He's with Miss Winstone

Ed: That's what you think.

Cam: Five minutes more, please.

The girls shrug and sit on the bed. The boys begin to ready themselves for bed. Cam brings Seb aside.

Seb: What do you want?

Cam: I think you know.

Jasmin: We really got to go soon.

Ed: Do you want to kiss us goodnight.

Georgia: Actually...no.

Cam: Not long, guys. Sharp'll be back soon.

Ben: It was after that lesson, the one where he tore my work up, that I started getting it from the other teachers – not all, but especially in rugby. Didn't realise it at first. But it's obvious now. The bell went and we started to leave. The chairs were out. Cooper! I turned slowly towards him, I'd had enough. Cooper – where are you going? Geography Sir – it's my next lesson. Are you being impudent Cooper? No sir, I've got to go, I'll be late. Your chair's out Cooper. They all are sir. *(Pause)* The silence was drowning me. What did you say? They're all out, sir. I wanted to hit him, but my throat was clogging up. It was like I'd swallowed a conker and it was lodged right there. I wanted to tell him what to do, but the words couldn't get out. Tears stinging my eyes, but not upset. Why are you crying Cooper? I'm not.

Then I saw that he was enjoying it. Come on Cooper, he said, I'm not that bad. Come on...

Ed: He tried it on me... *(He becomes aware of the looking, and then, sounding vulnerable)* just once...

Pause

Cam: I wish I was at the sing song. Round the jolly old camp fire. You are a lot, you really are.

He begins to sing; the others join in and a dance begins. Except Georgia, who just watches

There were eggs, eggs, eggs with hairy legs,

In the stores,

In the stores,

There were eggs, eggs, eggs with hairy legs,

In the Quartermaster's stores. *(Behind the Door)*

Chorus: (after each verse)

My eyes are dim, I cannot see,

I have not brought my specs with me,

I have - not - brought - my - specs - with - me!

Alex begins to see how manic it is getting, and he gradually withdraws

There was cheese, cheese, cheese with knobbly knees....

There was ham, ham, floating with the spam ....

From his rucksack Cam produces a knife. There is

silence.

Cam: Who's it going to be eh? *He points the knife*

one at a time, Alex is terrified no reason Alex, I think,

you're unique here.

Alex: What about you?

Cam: Me, I'm not here at all.

There was bread, bread, harder than your head ....

There were fleas, fleas, eating all the peas ....

The door opens and they look and freeze

Ed: Five minutes I said – Cooper.

Cam: Yes Sir, Mr Sharp Sir...

Jasmin: Come on...

Georgia: Wait!

Cam: This is the moment...

(He starts the song again, the others join in. Cam looks hard at The Teacher)

There was gravy, gravy, enough to float the navy....

There was butter, butter, running down the gutter ....

(Song continues, repeated if necessary)

Cam: Come to say goodnight Sir.

Will: Don't scare her like that...

Jasmin: I want to go...

Ed: Did we have it wrong, sir?

Alex: What? *He is almost crying now at the madness around him*

Cam: Too late now sir...

Cam: Me sir? I'm just me. It's just how I am, just like the others sir.

Cam: Not time enough sir.

Ben grabs the knife and advances hard

Cam: Go on...

He lifts his arm back swings – stops. There is a moment's pause.

Cam: Seb!

Seb grabs Ben's arm and the knife. He slashes at Will then hard three times into Ed.

Notes for Directors

Song suggestions: Either these have been accompanied by on stage musicians from cast, or sung unaccompanied. It is fine to replace the songs with ones of the Director's own choice. These particularly ones were chosen because they were:

> Out of copyright
>
> Easy to get hold of
>
> Easy to learn
>
> Easy to sing
>
> Fitted in with the 'campire' theme

Songs

Hush Little Baby (P4)

On Ilkley Moor b'tat (P7)

Gin Gan Goolie (P10)

Barbara Allen (P12)

She'll be coming round the mountain (P15)

The Quartermaster's Store (P23)

For some productions a chorus of campfire singers supported the on stage singers with the songs

Props

Minimal – P16 with CAMERON – rucksack containing enough bars of chocolate for all but one of the cast and a knife

Set

A bare, claustrophobic set was used in the Edinburgh Fringe productions. Enough hard chairs for most of the cast. We also had instruments on the stage for the cast to use

Printed in Great Britain
by Amazon